WITHDRAWN

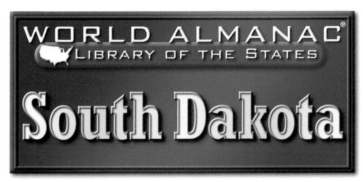

WORLD ALMANAC® · LIBRARY OF THE STATES

South Dakota

THE MOUNT RUSHMORE STATE

by Kris Hirschmann

WORLD ALMANAC® LIBRARY

Please visit our web site at: **www.worldalmanaclibrary.com**
**For a free color catalog describing World Almanac® Library's list of high-quality books
and multimedia programs, call 1-800-848-2928 (USA) or 1-800-387-3178 (Canada).
World Almanac® Library's fax: (414) 332-3567.**

Library of Congress Cataloging-in-Publication Data

Hirschmann, Kris, 1967-
    South Dakota, the Mount Rushmore State / by Kris Hirschmann.
      p. cm. — (World Almanac Library of the states)
    Includes bibliographical references and index.
    Summary: Presents the history, geography, people, government, economy,
social life and customs, and state events and attractions of South Dakota.
    ISBN 0-8368-5160-9 (lib. bdg.)
    ISBN 0-8368-5331-8 (softcover)
    1. South Dakota—Juvenile literature. [1. South Dakota.] I. Title. II. Series.
F651.3.H57   2003
978.3—dc21   2002043142

First published in 2003 by
World Almanac® Library
330 West Olive Street, Suite 100
Milwaukee, WI 53212 USA

Copyright © 2003 by World Almanac® Library.

A Creative Media Applications Production
Design: Alan Barnett, Inc.
Copy editor: Laurie Lieb
Fact checker: Joan Verniero
Photo researcher: Jamey O'Quinn
World Almanac® Library project editor: Tim Paulson
World Almanac® Library editors: Mary Dykstra, Gustav Gedatus, Jacqueline Laks Gorman,
  Lyman Lyons
World Almanac® Library art direction: Tammy Gruenewald
World Almanac® Library graphic designers: Scott M. Krall, Melissa Valuch

Photo credits: pp. 4-5 © Layne Kennedy/CORBIS; p. 6 © Roy Morsch/CORBIS; p. 6 © Annie
Griffiths Belt/CORBIS; p. 6 © Royalty-Free/CORBIS; p. 7 © Jim Richardson/CORBIS; p. 7
© South Dakota Tourism; p. 9 © Hulton Archive/Getty Images; p. 10 © Hulton Archive/Getty
Images; p. 11 © Bettmann/CORBIS; p. 12 © Royalty-Free/CORBIS; p. 13 © Bettmann/CORBIS;
p. 14 © Hulton Archive/Getty Images; p. 15 © AP/Wide World Photos; p. 17 © AP/Wide World
Photos; p. 18 © Lalage Johnstone; Eye Ubiquitous/CORBIS; p. 19 © Dave G. Houser/CORBIS;
p. 20 (left) © Getty/Photodisc; p. 20 (center) © Getty/Photodisc; p. 20 (right) © Layne
Kennedy/CORBIS; p. 21 (left) © Tim Thompson/CORBIS; p. 21 (center) © Dave G.
Houser/CORBIS; p. 21 (right) © Layne Kennedy/CORBIS; p. 23 © AP/Wide World Photos; p. 26
© Peter Johnson/CORBIS; p. 27 © Getty/Photodisc; p. 29 © AP/Wide World Photos; p. 31
© AP/Wide World Photos; p. 31 © AP/Wide World Photos; p. 32 © Tom Nebbia/CORBIS; p. 33
© Royalty-Free/CORBIS; p. 34 © Nik Wheeler/CORBIS; p. 35 © Jay Dickman/CORBIS; p. 36
© Nik Wheeler/CORBIS; p. 37 © Tom Bean/CORBIS; p. 37 © Getty/Photodisc; p. 38 © CORBIS;
p. 39 © Bettmann/CORBIS; p. 39 © Bettmann/CORBIS; p. 40 © AP/Wide World Photos; p. 41
© AP/Wide World Photos; p. 41 © Bettmann/CORBIS; p. 41 © John-Marshall Mantel/CORBIS;
pp. 42-43 © Hulton Archive/Getty Images; p. 44 © Layne Kennedy/CORBIS; p. 44 © Royalty-
Free/CORBIS; p. 45 © Kevin Fleming/CORBIS; p. 45 © Getty/Photodisc

Printed in the United States of America

2 3 4 5 6 7 8 9 07 06 05 04 03

South Dakota

INTRODUCTION	4
ALMANAC	6
HISTORY	8
THE PEOPLE	16
THE LAND	20
ECONOMY & COMMERCE	24
POLITICS & GOVERNMENT	28
CULTURE & LIFESTYLE	32
NOTABLE PEOPLE	38
TIME LINE	42
STATE EVENTS & ATTRACTIONS	44
MORE ABOUT SOUTH DAKOTA	46
INDEX	47

A Balancing Act

Thousands of years ago, South Dakota's prairies were home to vast herds of free-roaming bison. The bison attracted the area's first human residents — Native peoples who followed the bison and hunted them for food, clothing, shelter, and other necessities.

The great prairies of the West eventually attracted other humans, too. As America became increasingly populated by white people of European descent, settlers flocked to the plains to establish farms and ranches on South Dakota's wide-open expanses. The result was decades of conflict between settlers and Native residents as both sides fought for control of the prairies. In the end, the settlers' interests won out, and most of South Dakota was transformed into agricultural land.

Since its establishment as an agricultural powerhouse, South Dakota has been one of America's most important farming and ranching states. Like other U.S. states, however, South Dakota has undergone an economic transition in the decades since the mid-1900s. Service industries (industries such as finance, trade, and tourism that sell services rather than goods) and manufacturing have overtaken agriculture as the state's most important economic sectors. Finance in particular is a mainstay of South Dakota's economy. Tourism is also important to the state's economic health.

Despite this economic shift, South Dakota is still an agricultural state at heart. About 90 percent of the state's land area is covered by farms and ranches. Many of the state's residents work in agriculture-related industries.

South Dakota has the nation's third-highest percentage of Native American residents. The state is therefore a crucial part of any national debate about Native rights, living conditions, or other important issues. Today, as in previous centuries, balancing the needs and desires of farmers, ranchers, and Native residents (as well as the state's growing professional population) is a task that both occupies and defines the state of South Dakota.

▶ Map of South Dakota showing the interstate highway system, as well as major cities and waterways.

▼ South Dakota's landscape consists mostly of rolling grasslands called prairies. Most of the state's prairies support farms and ranches.

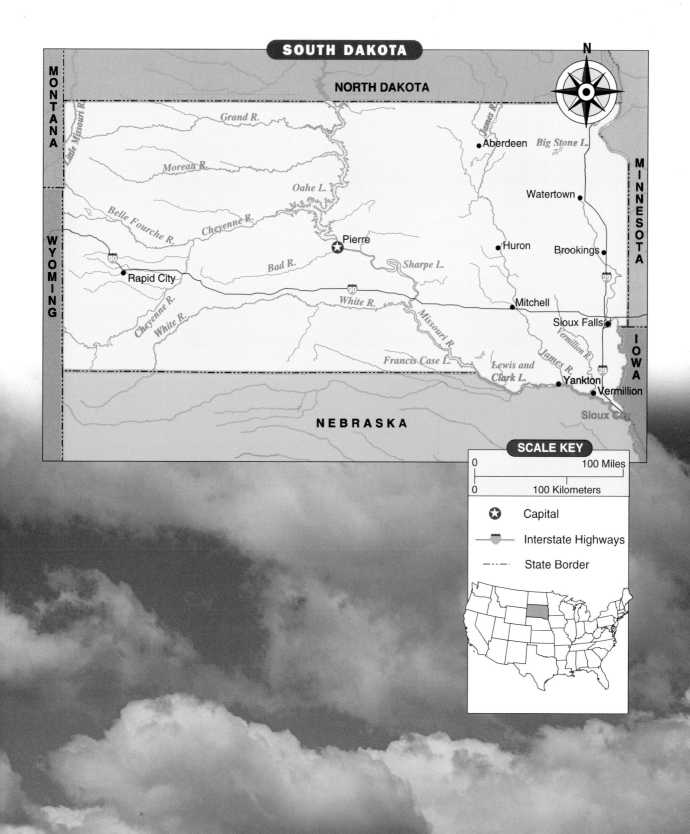

SOUTH DAKOTA

MONTANA

NORTH DAKOTA

N

WYOMING

MINNESOTA

Little Missouri R.

Grand R.

Moreau R.

Oahe L.

Belle Fourche R.

Cheyenne R.

⭐ Pierre

Aberdeen •

Big Stone L.

Watertown •

• Huron

Brookings •

IOWA

90

• Rapid City

Bad R.

Sharpe L.

Cheyenne R.

White R.

White R.

Missouri R.

• Mitchell

Sioux Falls •

29

Francis Case L.

Lewis and Clark L.

Vermillion R.

James R.

29

Yankton •

• Vermillion

Sioux City

NEBRASKA

SCALE KEY

0 — 100 Miles

0 — 100 Kilometers

⭐ Capital

Interstate Highways

–··– State Border

Fast Facts

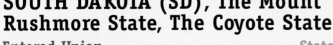

SOUTH DAKOTA (SD), The Mount Rushmore State, The Coyote State

Entered Union

November 2, 1889 (40th state)

Capital	Population
Pierre	13,876

Total Population (2000)

754,844 (46th most populous state) — *Between 1990 and 2000, the state's population increased 8.5 percent.*

Largest Cities	Population
Sioux Falls	123,975
Rapid City	59,607
Aberdeen	24,658
Watertown	20,237
Brookings	18,504

Land Area

75,885 square miles (196,542 square kilometers) (16th largest state)

State Motto

"Under God the People Rule"

State Song

"Hail! South Dakota" *by Deecort Hammitt, adopted in 1943*

State Slogan

Great Faces. Great Places. — *This slogan refers to the famous faces on Mount Rushmore and all the other interesting people and places across South Dakota.*

State Bird

Chinese ring-necked pheasant

State Animal

Coyote

State Fish

Walleye — *The walleye is the most sought-after game fish in South Dakota.*

State Insect

Honeybee — *The honeybee was adopted as state insect because of its importance to the state's economy. South Dakota is a leader in honey production.*

State Flower

Pasqueflower — *The blooming of the lavender pasqueflower is one of the first signs of spring in South Dakota.*

State Tree

Black Hills spruce

State Fossil

Triceratops

State Gemstone

Fairburn agate — *This semiprecious stone was first discovered near Fairburn.*

State Mineral

Rose quartz

PLACES TO VISIT

Badlands National Park, *southwestern South Dakota*
Rocky cliffs, spires, canyons, and other formations make this national park unique.

Corn Palace, *Mitchell*
This building is sometimes called "the world's biggest bird feeder" because it is decorated with three thousand bushels of corn.

Mount Rushmore National Memorial, *near Custer*
Carved into a granite hillside, the Mount Rushmore National Memorial is one of America's most recognized attractions. It features the faces of former U.S. presidents George Washington, Thomas Jefferson, Theodore Roosevelt, and Abraham Lincoln.

For other places and events, see p. 44.

BIGGEST, BEST, AND MOST

- South Dakota has more bison than any other U.S. state. An estimated eight thousand of these animals are scattered among South Dakota's parks and private ranches.

- Sioux Falls consistently ranks as one of "America's Top 20 Best Places to Live" on an annual *Money* magazine list.

- The largest gold mine in the United States was the Homestake Mining Company in Lead, which closed in 2001.

STATE FIRSTS

- **1889** South Dakota became the first state to adopt the initiative, a process that allows voters to propose and vote on new laws.

- **1892** The world's first gasoline-powered tractor went into service in Langford.

- **1973** Democrat James Abourezk of South Dakota became the first Arab-American elected to the U.S. Senate.

Flaming Waters

The Flaming Fountain Memorial, located in the capital city of Pierre, is dedicated to South Dakotans who have fought for their country. The fountain is fed by well water that contains natural gas, which bursts into flames if ignited. The

Photo by South Dakota Tourism

waters of the fountain burn perpetually to honor South Dakota's soldiers. People visiting the Flaming Fountain Memorial can also pay tribute to South Dakota's veterans at the South Dakota Korean and Vietnam War Memorial, which overlooks the fountain.

Mammoths on Display

Hot Springs is the home of the Mammoth Site, one of the world's most extensive fossil displays. More than fifty mammoth skeletons have been unearthed at this site, along with the skeletons of ancient bears, camels, llamas, wolves, and other creatures. Twenty-six thousand years ago, the Mammoth Site was probably a sinkhole that contained a warm spring. The spring attracted mammoths and other thirsty animals. Once the animals had descended into the sinkhole to drink the water, however, they could not climb back out. They eventually died of starvation. Over hundreds of years, the sinkhole filled with silt and sediment that protected the animals' remains and allowed them to turn into the magnificent fossils on display at the Mammoth Site today.

The Heart of the Plains

> Why, here was Dakota Territory about to become a state —
> yessir, an inseparable part of the very Union itself.
> Everybody was excited about it. They held meetings,
> they talked meetings, they discussed politics until
> they got madder than blazes.
> — *Author O. E. Rölvaag,* Peder Victorious, *1982*

The first residents of the South Dakota region were the Paleo-Indians. Anthropologists believe that the Paleo-Indians descended from people who crossed a land bridge that once connected present-day Siberia to North America. The earliest artifacts of the South Dakota area's Paleo-Indians date back to around 8000 B.C.

The Paleo-Indians eventually disappeared for unknown reasons. Some scientists believe that a drought might have forced them to leave the area. Others think that a plague wiped them out. Whatever the reason, the South Dakota region was left without human inhabitants.

Ancestors of South Dakota's modern Native peoples began arriving in the early 1500s. The first Natives to arrive were the Arikara, and the Cheyenne came later. The last major Native group to arrive was the Sioux. The Sioux began moving into the South Dakota area in the early 1700s and soon dominated the region.

The Early European Years

The first Europeans to explore the South Dakota area were probably brothers François and Louis Joseph de La Vérendrye. These French explorers traveled through the West in 1742 and 1743. Near what is now the city of Pierre, they buried a lead plaque claiming the South Dakota region for France. The area became part of a French territory called Louisiana, which included most of the midsection of the continental United States.

In 1803, French Emperor Napoleon Bonaparte sold the Louisiana Territory to the United States for $15 million.

Native Americans of South Dakota

Arikara

Cheyenne

Sioux

DID YOU KNOW?

The Sioux presently living in western South Dakota call themselves the Lakota. Those living in eastern South Dakota call themselves the Dakota. Both words mean "ally."

This sale, which became known as the Louisiana Purchase, doubled the size of the United States. It also transferred all of the region that is now South Dakota to U.S. possession.

Lewis and Clark

Following the Louisiana Purchase, U.S. President Thomas Jefferson organized an Expedition to explore the nation's new property. He appointed two U.S. Army officers, Meriwether Lewis and William Clark, to lead the Expedition. In 1804, Lewis and Clark's group (called the Corps of Discovery) left St. Louis, Missouri, and headed up the Missouri River. They reached the area that is now South Dakota in August 1804 and spent about two months crossing the region. After traveling all the way to the Pacific Ocean, Lewis and Clark returned to South Dakota in 1806.

As they traveled, Lewis and Clark kept detailed journals about the things they saw and experienced on their journey. These journals were eventually published and widely read.

Settlers Arrive

Encouraged by Lewis and Clark's reports of the many valuable pelt animals in the South Dakota region, trappers and hunters soon headed west to seek their fortunes. In 1817,

▼ In this painting by Frederic Remington, Lewis and Clark's party sets up camp on its journey of discovery and exploration.

French trader Joseph La Framboise opened the area's first permanent trading post on the banks of the Missouri River near present-day Pierre. Trade was slow at first but picked up in 1831 after the steamboat *Yellowstone* began making regular trips to Fort Tecumseh, as the post was then called. (In 1832 the post was renamed Fort Pierre.)

The *Yellowstone* did more than just encourage trade. It also brought artists, explorers, missionaries, and other visitors to the South Dakota area. When these visitors returned east, their stories encouraged more and more people to travel to America's new frontier. Farmers, ranchers, and other permanent residents soon appeared in the area.

Conflict with the Sioux

As larger numbers of settlers arrived in the South Dakota region, resentment grew among the area's Native peoples, particularly the Sioux. White hunters were killing huge numbers of bison, an animal whose hide, flesh, blood, and bones were used by the Sioux for many purposes. Non-Native farmers and ranchers were also ruining traditional Sioux hunting grounds. The Sioux became increasingly angry and finally began to attack isolated settlers in an

▼ Sioux hunters on horseback pursue a herd of bison in this painting by Charles Marion Russell.

attempt to drive the intruders away.

In 1851, the U.S. government and some Sioux tribes tried to stop the fighting by signing the Laramie Treaty. This treaty granted 60 million acres (24,282,000 hectares) of land to the Sioux and established tribal borders. However, the fighting continued. In 1858, the Yankton Treaty made another attempt at peace through the purchase of fourteen million acres (5,665,800 ha) of land from another Sioux band. The treaty also moved tribe members onto reservations. For a short time, these actions brought peace to the South Dakota region.

The Sodbusters

In 1861, the U.S. Congress established Dakota Territory. This territory included what is now North and South Dakota, much of Wyoming and Montana, and a small part of Idaho. (The original Dakota Territory, however, was short-lived. In 1868, Montana, Wyoming, and Idaho were incorporated into other territories, leaving only present-day North and South Dakota.) Eager to populate the new territory, Congress passed the Homestead Act in 1862. This act entitled settlers to 160 acres (65 ha) of free land if they built a home and lived on the land for at least five years.

In response, settlers flocked to the area. They soon discovered, however, that building homes in Dakota Territory was not easy. Most areas had few trees or other construction materials. Therefore, many prospective farmers were forced to cut thick strips of sod and stack them like bricks to build shelters. These earthen shacks were called "soddies," and the people who lived in them were called "sodbusters."

Even after a soddy was built, there was no guarantee of success for a Dakota farmer. One dry year could ruin a farm. Huge swarms of grasshoppers sometimes ate entire crops, prairie tornadoes destroyed homes, and fierce winter

Wovoka

Although Paiute holy man Wovoka spent most of his life in Nevada, he had an important effect on the history of South Dakota. Born around 1856 as the son of a well-known medicine man, young Wovoka had dreams and visions that marked him as a holy man in his own right. The turning point in Wovoka's life came in January 1889, when he regained consciousness after several days in a coma caused by an illness. Wovoka said he had had a spiritual vision showing him how to free Natives across the West from the settlers' domination. This goal, however, could be achieved only by following a special ritual called the Ghost Dance. Native tribes across the nation, including the Sioux of South Dakota, quickly adopted the dance. Unfortunately, many Natives misinterpreted Wovoka's essentially peaceful message and began to act more aggressively toward settlers. In South Dakota, Wokova's Ghost Dance and the changing Sioux attitudes led to the massacre at Wounded Knee.

blizzards discouraged all but the hardiest farming families. Only about 40 percent of all Dakota Territory settlers lasted the entire five years and earned their free land.

More Conflict with the Natives

While the sodbusters settled the plains, conflict between the settlers and Dakota Territory's Native peoples continued. In 1868, Congress and the Sioux tried once more to ease hostilities with the Fort Laramie Treaty. This treaty established the Great Sioux Reservation, which included the Black Hills region. It also gave the Sioux possession of a large portion of land in Dakota Territory, including the region west of the Missouri in South Dakota. Peace reigned once again.

But this peace did not last long. In 1873, the Northern Pacific Railroad began planning a route through the Black Hills to reach gold rush country in Montana. The proposed railway route violated the Fort Laramie Treaty, and the Sioux reacted violently. Native warriors attacked the Northern Pacific's surveyors and, later, any white miners or travelers crossing the land.

In response to the Sioux attacks, U.S. Army troops were sent to Dakota Territory. A series of battles forced the Natives onto smaller and smaller parcels of land.

Massacre at Wounded Knee

In 1889, Congress introduced yet another treaty designed to both pacify and restrict the Native tribes of the West. Called the Great Sioux Agreement, the treaty established six reservation areas within South Dakota. It also opened up more than 9 million new acres (3.6 million ha) of land to white settlement.

Unhappy with the conditions they were being forced to accept, more and more Natives began practicing a religious ritual called the Ghost Dance, which was supposed to make the settlers disappear. U.S. troops were alarmed by the Ghost Dance and tried to stop it whenever they could. Tension between the troops and the Natives grew as the dance became more and more popular and widespread.

▼ The Wounded Knee Massacre Memorial commemorates the 1890 massacre of nearly three hundred Sioux by U.S. soldiers.

Matters came to a head on December 29, 1890, at a Native encampment near Wounded Knee Creek in southwest South Dakota. Surrounded by U.S. soldiers, a Native brave began a Ghost Dance. The nervous soldiers pulled out their guns and shot the dancer, then other tribe members who happened to be standing nearby. Soon nearly three hundred Natives, including women and children, were dead.

The massacre at Wounded Knee was one of the saddest and most brutal episodes in the Indian wars of the West. Historians feel that this incident was responsible for finally breaking the Natives' spirit and ending their resistance to the never-ending stream of white settlers. After Wounded Knee, the Natives of the West allowed themselves to be moved onto reservations. There they worked to adjust to the new way of life required of them by the expanding settler population.

▲ "Calamity Jane" traveled the frontier in men's clothing. She was skillful with a rifle and known as a sharpshooter.

The Great Dakota Boom

During the Indian wars period, Dakota Territory's non-Native population increased rapidly. The new settlers were attracted partly by Dakota's farm and ranch land. Just as important, however, was the discovery of gold. In 1874, a story in a Chicago newspaper claimed that gold was "everywhere" in Dakota Territory's Black Hills. Seemingly overnight, a flood of miners appeared to hunt for riches. Mining towns sprang up to support the growing miner population.

Dakota's miners brought a fresh vitality to the region. They also brought railways and other services needed to support the area's many new towns.

Becoming a State

Between the miners, the farmers, and the ranchers, Dakota Territory was becoming well established. The area's growing population was eager for statehood. Accordingly, Dakota Territory began to work toward becoming a U.S. state. Public opinion was divided, however, about how this should happen. Some people wanted all of Dakota Territory to be a single state. Others wanted to split the territory into two states — North Dakota and South Dakota.

Several constitutions were written and sent to Congress for approval, but Dakota Territory was denied statehood again and again. Finally, however, Congress agreed to allow

The Wildest Town in the West

Gold was discovered near the town of Deadwood in 1876. Soon prospectors began arriving in droves, changing the sleepy city into a rowdy community where drinking, gambling, gunfights, and other rough activities reigned. Deadwood quickly earned a reputation as one of the wildest towns in the West. This mining community was the temporary home of some of the West's most famous characters, including Wild Bill Hickok and Martha "Calamity Jane" Burke.

North Dakota and South Dakota to join the Union as separate states. On November 2, 1889, President Benjamin Harrison signed bills that made North Dakota the nation's thirty-ninth state and South Dakota the nation's fortieth state.

Good Times, Bad Times

Becoming a state brought South Dakota many rights and privileges. However, it did not make life any easier for South Dakotans. Farmers still struggled with blizzards, droughts, grasshoppers, and other perils of life on the plains. Times were hard, and residents of the brand-new state fought to survive.

The state's economy picked up during the years of U.S. involvement in World War I (1917–1918), when demand rose for South Dakota's crops, livestock, and minerals. Unfortunately, the boom did not last much beyond the war years. As demand fell after the war, the state's economy worsened. Then the Great Depression of the 1930s hit, crippling the national economy and hurting South Dakota even further. The state's population fell as thousands of South Dakotans left to look for better living conditions elsewhere.

The bad times continued until late in 1941, when the United States entered World War II. Once again there was a market for South Dakota's goods. Money poured into the state and people prospered.

After World War II ended in 1945, the U.S. government started projects that were designed to solve some of South Dakota's problems, particularly those related to the area's farming and ranching industries. Four dams were built along the Missouri River to control flooding and provide electrical power. The dams also made it easier for South Dakota farmers to irrigate their fields.

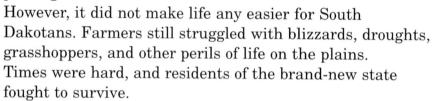

▲ A South Dakota sodbuster sits outside his earthen home, called a soddy. Trees were scarce on the prairie, so early settlers used blocks of earth and grass to build their houses. Over the years, a farmer would work to replace his soddy with a more permanent structure.

DID YOU KNOW?

When President Benjamin Harrison signed the bills that established North and South Dakota as states, he shuffled the papers so no one would know which was signed first. North Dakota was named the thirty-ninth state because it came ahead of South Dakota alphabetically. However, no one knows which state was *really* first.

South Dakota Today

Today, agriculture continues to dominate the South Dakota lifestyle; most of the state's land is dedicated to farming and ranching interests, and many South Dakotans work in these industries. Modern techniques have made the agricultural life a bit more predictable, but it is still not easy.

Native issues are still important in South Dakota as well. In 1973, a group called the American Indian Movement (AIM) held a seventy-one-day protest at Wounded Knee on the Pine Ridge Reservation to highlight the miserable living conditions of the area's residents. The AIM rally did not solve the reservation's problems, but the group did get a commitment from the U.S. government to meet and discuss possible solutions.

South Dakota's Native peoples scored another victory in 1980, when the U.S. Supreme Court ruled that the U.S. government had illegally seized the Sioux's Black Hills land in 1876. The Supreme Court ordered the government to pay the Sioux $122.5 million for the land it had taken. Some Sioux groups, however, refused the payment, preferring the return of the land instead. So far this request has not been granted, and the fight over the Black Hills continues today.

Despite these conflicts, South Dakota is generally a peaceful agricultural state where farming and ranching concerns continue to take center stage.

Where the Buffalo Roam

Before white pioneers, hunters, and soldiers arrived in the Dakota region, an estimated sixty million bison roamed the prairies of the West. Within one hundred years of the whites' arrival, however, fewer than a thousand bison remained. After this brush with extinction, the bison was given protected status. Today the U.S. bison population has rebounded to more than two hundred fifty thousand. South Dakota is home to more public bison herds than any other U.S. state. South Dakota's bison can be found in Custer State Park and Wind Cave National Park, on Indian reservations, and on private farms and ranches.

Below: Today, herds of American bison roam the prairies of South Dakota, protected from hunters.

Living the Simple Life

> More Americans than ever, well over 70 percent, now live in urban areas and tend to see Plains land as empty. What they really mean is devoid of human presence. . . . They may wonder why a person would choose to live in such a barren place, let alone love it.
>
> — *Author Kathleen Norris,* Dakota: A Spiritual Geography, *1993*

With 754,844 people spread across 75,885 square miles (196,542 sq km) of land, South Dakota is among the most sparsely populated U.S. states. In 2000 the state had just 9.9 residents per square mile (3.8 residents per sq km). Only Alaska, Wyoming, Montana, and North Dakota had lower population densities.

Most of South Dakota's people live in the eastern half of the state. Of South Dakota's ten largest cities, nine — Sioux Falls, Aberdeen, Watertown, Brookings, Mitchell, Pierre, Yankton, Huron, and Vermillion — are found east of the Missouri River. Together, residents of these cities account for about one-third of South Dakota's population. Only Rapid City is located west of the Missouri.

Age Distribution in South Dakota
(2000 Census)

0–4	51,069
5–19	176,412
20–24	52,802
25–44	206,399
45–64	160,031
65 & over	108,131

Across One Hundred Years

South Dakota's three largest foreign-born groups for 1890 and 1990

1890			1990		
Norway	Germany	Russia	Canada	Germany	United Kingdom
19,257	18,188	12,398	892	816	467

Total state population: 328,808
Total foreign-born: 91,055 (27.7%)

Total state population: 696,004
Total foreign-born: 7,731 (1.1%)

Patterns of Immigration

The total number of people who immigrated to South Dakota in 1998 was 356. Of that number, the largest immigrant groups were from Mexico (10.1%), the Philippines (5.3%), and Russia (4.5%).

▶ Indian artist Paha Ska, an elder of the Oglala Sioux from the Pine Ridge Reservation, holds a Presidential Peace Medallion presented by President Thomas Jefferson. The medallion was given to Native leaders by the Lewis and Clark Expedition in 1803. Paha Ska visits schools and talks about the Native American heritage of South Dakota.

Most South Dakotans have European roots. German ancestry is by far the most common; 40 percent of all South Dakotans are descended from German immigrants. South Dakotans with roots in Scandinavian countries, including Norway, Sweden, and Denmark, are the next largest group. Irish, English, and Dutch backgrounds are common as well.

Native Americans make up 8.3 percent of the state's population. Other minorities, including African Americans, Asians, and Hispanics, account for just a small portion of the state's ethnic mix.

The Native Population

In 2000, South Dakota's Native American population numbered 62,283. Nearly all of these Native Americans had Sioux ancestry.

About three-fourths of South Dakota's Native residents live on one of the state's nine reservations. The remaining one-fourth are scattered throughout nonreservation areas. The largest reservations in terms of population are the Pine Ridge and Rosebud Reservations in the southwestern

Heritage and Background, South Dakota   **Year 2000**

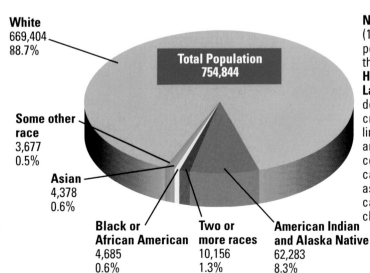

▶ Here is a look at the racial backgrounds of South Dakotans today. South Dakota ranks forty-fifth among all U.S. states with regard to African Americans as a percentage of the population.

Native Hawaiian and Other Pacific Islander
261
0.03%

White
669,404
88.7%

Total Population
754,844

Some other race
3,677
0.5%

Asian
4,378
0.6%

Black or African American
4,685
0.6%

Two or more races
10,156
1.3%

American Indian and Alaska Native
62,283
8.3%

Note: 1.4% (10,903) of the population identify themselves as **Hispanic** or **Latino,** a cultural designation that crosses racial lines. Hispanics and Latinos are counted in this category as well as the racial category of their choice.

portion of the state. The Standing Rock, Yankton, and Cheyenne River Reservations are also large.

One objective of South Dakota's reservations is to preserve the Sioux way of life by creating Native communities and helping to keep old traditions alive. However, reservation life is not easy. Native reservations have long represented U.S. government policies of confinement and neglect, leading in many cases to poor living conditions for reservation residents. High school and college graduation rates are low compared to those of the general population. Unemployment is a serious problem, and most people's incomes fall well below the poverty level. Native-run casinos and other businesses bring much-needed jobs and cash into many of South Dakota's reservations.

Educational Levels of South Dakota Workers (age 25 and over)	
Less than 9th grade	35,421
9th to 12th grade, no diploma	37,759
High school graduate, including equivalency	156,006
Some college, no degree or associate degree	143,161
Bachelor's degree	73,563
Graduate or professional degree	28,449

▼ Traditional red barns along South Dakota's back roads dot its prairies and agricultural landscape.

Religion

South Dakotans are overwhelmingly Christian. In 1990, nearly 70 percent of the state's residents were members of a Christian organization, making South Dakota the fourth most Christian state in America.

The largest single religious organization in South Dakota is the Lutheran Church. The second largest is the Roman Catholic Church. Protestant groups include Methodists, Baptists, and Presbyterians. The Church of Latter-day Saints also has a presence, and a few Jewish synagogues are located in major cities.

▲ After the Civil War, churches sprang up throughout the prairie. The churches were often small, but they helped build a sense of community for early settlers.

Education

South Dakota's first school opened in 1860 in Bon Homme County. Just two years later, in 1862, the territorial government established a school code and a common school district. Dakota Territory's first superintendent of public instruction was appointed in 1864. South Dakota has been strongly committed to public education ever since. This commitment is demonstrated by the fact that ever since it became a state, South Dakota has elected a commissioner of school and public lands as one of its seven main executive-branch officers.

Over the years, South Dakota's educational system has grown along with the state's population. Today South Dakota has more than 750 public elementary and secondary schools with an enrollment of approximately 130,000 students. The school system consistently ranks among the best in the nation in terms of graduation percentages and students' scores on standardized tests.

In addition to its elementary and secondary schools, South Dakota runs seven public colleges and universities. Major state-run schools include South Dakota State University in Brookings and the University of South Dakota in Vermillion. Private schools of note include Dakota Wesleyan University in Mitchell, Augustana College and the University of Sioux Falls in Sioux Falls, and Mount Marty College in Yankton. Community colleges and Native American–run colleges, include the South Dakota School of Mines and Technology in Rapid City and Sisseton's Wahpeton Community College.

The Hutterites

In addition to its major religions, South Dakota is also the home of a unique group called the Hutterites. There are about fifty Hutterite colonies in South Dakota, each with sixty to one hundred members. The German-speaking Hutterites adhere to a strict dress code and believe in communal ownership of property. They maintain a simple, religiously based way of life and resist many of the customs of the modern world.

Wide-Open Spaces

There was something else here that was not anywhere else.
It was an enormous stillness that made you feel still. . . .
Even the sounds of eating and talking could not touch
the enormous silence of this prairie.

— *Author Laura Ingalls Wilder*, By the Shores of Silver Lake, *1941*

With a total land area of 75,885 square miles (196,542 sq km), South Dakota is the sixteenth-largest U.S. state. It is mostly rectangular in shape, with jagged river-defined borders at the northeastern and southeastern corners. South Dakota is bordered by North Dakota to the north, Nebraska to the south, Minnesota and Iowa to the east, and Montana and Wyoming to the west.

Land elevations in South Dakota range from a high of 7,242 feet (2,207 meters) at Harney Peak in the southwest to a low of 966 feet (294 m) at Big Stone Lake in the northeast.

Rivers and Lakes

The mighty Missouri River flows all the way through South Dakota from its northern to southern borders. Major tributaries of the Missouri include the Big Sioux, Vermillion, and James Rivers in the east and the Grand, Moreau, Cheyenne, Bad, and White Rivers in the west.

South Dakota's biggest lakes are part of the Missouri River. Dams on the river back up the waters into Lewis and Clark Lake and Lakes Oahe, Francis Case, and

Highest Point
Harney Peak
7,242 feet (2,207 m)
above sea level

▼ *From left to right:* a rolling South Dakota prairie; the Badlands; a lightning strike showing extreme weather; sunflowers ready to be harvested; the world-famous Walls Drug Store; a road winding through the South Dakota prairie.

Sharpe. Together these four lakes are known as the Great Lakes of South Dakota. The state also has hundreds of smaller lakes, mostly in the northeast that were created during an era when glaciers covered and gouged the land.

East vs. West

The Missouri River is not only South Dakota's largest waterway, but it also divides the state into two distinct regions. The two regions are usually referred to as East River (which includes the land east of the Missouri) and West River (which includes the land west of the Missouri).

East River features low, rolling prairies, especially in the south. The southern part of East River also contains some of America's most fertile soil; most of South Dakota's farms are found in this area. The terrain is hillier to the north, where small lakes that are sometimes called "prairie potholes" dot the land.

The West River region has a very different character. Buttes (steep, rocky hills) jut up from the plains in the northern and central parts of the region. Grassy expanses can be found between the buttes, but dry weather gives the grasses a brown color for most of the year.

A major feature of West River is the Black Hills. Found in the far southwest, these mountains are covered with pine trees that look black from a distance. The Black Hills cover an area that is roughly 50 miles (80 km) wide and 120 miles (193 km) long. Also found in the southwest are the Badlands, South Dakota's most unusual natural feature. The Badlands are an area of colorful cliffs, spikes, canyons, and other rock formations that formed over millions of years when wind, rain, and other natural forces wore away soft rock and soil to expose harder parts.

Average January temperature
Rapid City: 22°F (-6°C)
Sioux Falls: 14°F (-10°C)

Average July temperature
Rapid City: 72°F (22°C)
Sioux Falls: 74°F (23°C)

Average yearly rainfall
Rapid City:
 16.6 inches (42.2 cm)
Sioux Falls:
 23.9 inches (60.7 cm)

Average yearly snowfall
Rapid City:
 39 inches (99.1 cm)
Sioux Falls:
 40 inches (101.6 cm)

DID YOU KNOW?

The geographic center of the fifty U.S. states is in South Dakota. This imaginary point is found near the city of Belle Fourche in the west-central region.

Largest Lakes

Lake Oahe
370,000 acres
 (149,739 hectares)

Lake Francis Case
60,000 acres
 (24,282 ha)

Lake Sharpe
30,000 acres (12,141 ha)

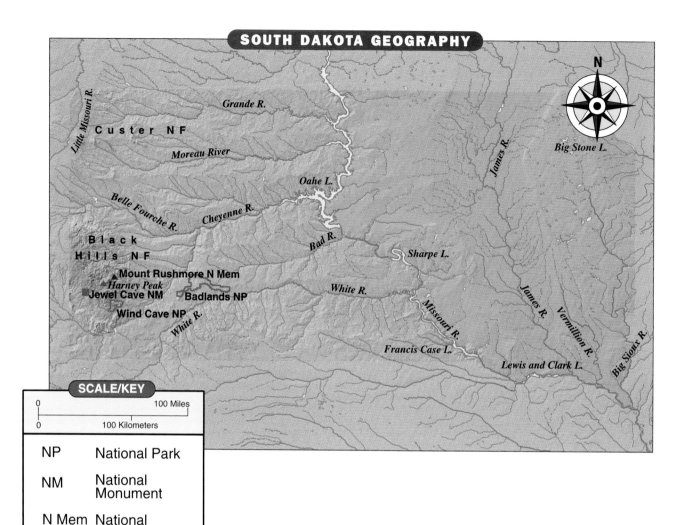

Little Missouri R.

Grande R.

Custer NF

Moreau River

Oahe L.

Belle Fourche R.

Cheyenne R.

Bad R.

Black Hills NF

Sharpe L.

▲ Mount Rushmore N Mem

Harney Peak

Jewel Cave NM ☐ Badlands NP

White R.

Wind Cave NP

White R.

Missouri R.

Francis Case L.

James R.

Big Stone L.

James R.

Vermillion R.

Big Sioux R.

Lewis and Clark L.

N

SCALE/KEY

0	100 Miles
0	100 Kilometers

NP	National Park
NM	National Monument
N Mem	National Memorial
NF	National Forest
▲	Highest Point
▲	Important Peaks
▨	Mountains

Climate

As far as its climate, South Dakota is a land of extremes. Summers tend to be hot and dry, especially in the south-central region. Winters are snowy and bone-chillingly cold, often bringing terrible blizzards with wind speeds above 70 miles (113 km) per hour.

High winds are common at other times of the year as well. The western part of the state in particular experiences strong, steady winds that blow nearly constantly. Many old wooden buildings in this part of South Dakota have been blown crooked by the unrelenting wind.

The Black Hills region sometimes experiences special winds called "chinooks." Born in the Pacific Ocean, these winds carry warm, dry air that can dramatically change a region's temperature. In South Dakota, air temperatures have been known to rise nearly 50 degrees Fahrenheit (28 degrees Celsius) in just minutes when a chinook blows.

Plants and Animals

Only about 3.5 percent of South Dakota is considered forest area. Most woods are found in the Custer National Forest in the northwest and the Black Hills National Forest in the southwest. Pine, spruce, aspen, and juniper trees grow in these areas.

In nonwooded areas, prairie grasses and wildflowers are the most common plants. Pasqueflowers, sunflowers, primroses, geraniums, and black-eyed Susans are just a few of the colorful flowers that decorate South Dakota's fields in the warm months of the year.

South Dakota has nearly ninety native mammals. Large mammals include coyotes (which give the state one of its nicknames), bighorn sheep, antelope, elk, and deer. The state is also home to several herds of bison that live and graze on protected lands. South Dakota's population of small mammals includes beavers, skunks, porcupines, and prairie dogs.

Many varieties of birds, fish, and reptiles live in South Dakota as well. About 350 bird species, forty-five reptile species, thirty fish species, and thousands of species of insects are also native to the state.

Major Rivers

Missouri River
2,315 miles (3,725 km)

James River
710 miles (1,142 km)

White River
507 miles (816 km)

Cheyenne River
527 miles (848 km)

▼ Antelope and other large animals sometimes travel along plowed highways to avoid the deep snows that cover South Dakota's open prairie as they search for food in winter.

From Farms to Finance

> For the nine-to-five crowd, work is something you do for 40 hours every week, making a clean break at the end of each day. . . . On a farm, the first 40 hours are used up by noon on Wednesday.
>
> — *Author Greg Latza,* Back on the Farm, *1999*

In South Dakota's earliest days, the state economy was based mostly on agriculture. Many of the state's first European settlers were sodbusters who came to the area just to work the soil.

Agriculture is still an extremely important part of the South Dakota landscape, both socially and economically. But today, South Dakota's economy is not as dependent on agriculture as it once was. As in most U.S. states, a shift has taken place in recent decades. Service industries (those in which services, not goods, are sold) are now the most important sector of South Dakota's economy. Manufacturing also contributes a significant percentage of South Dakota's gross state product (the total value of goods and services produced in the state).

Services

Finance is big business in South Dakota. The state is the home of many major financial institutions, including the massive Citicorp in Sioux Falls. As a group, South Dakota's banks and other financial organizations (including insurance companies) contributed 13.8 percent of the gross state product in 2000. Other major services included wholesale and retail trade; transportation and utilities; and real estate. Together, these industries accounted for 30.5 percent of South Dakota's state income in 2000.

South Dakota's government is also a large part of the services sector. In 2000, government activities generated 12.7 percent of the state's gross product. South Dakota's federal, state, local, and military workers are part of the

Top Employers (of workers age sixteen and over)
Services 40.4%
Wholesale and retail trade 15.3%
Manufacturing .11.1%
Agriculture, forestry, fisheries, and mining 8.1%
Finance, insurance, and real estate . . . 7.4%
Transportation, communications, and other utilities . . . 6.8%
Construction 6.3%
Federal, state, and local government (including military) 4.8%

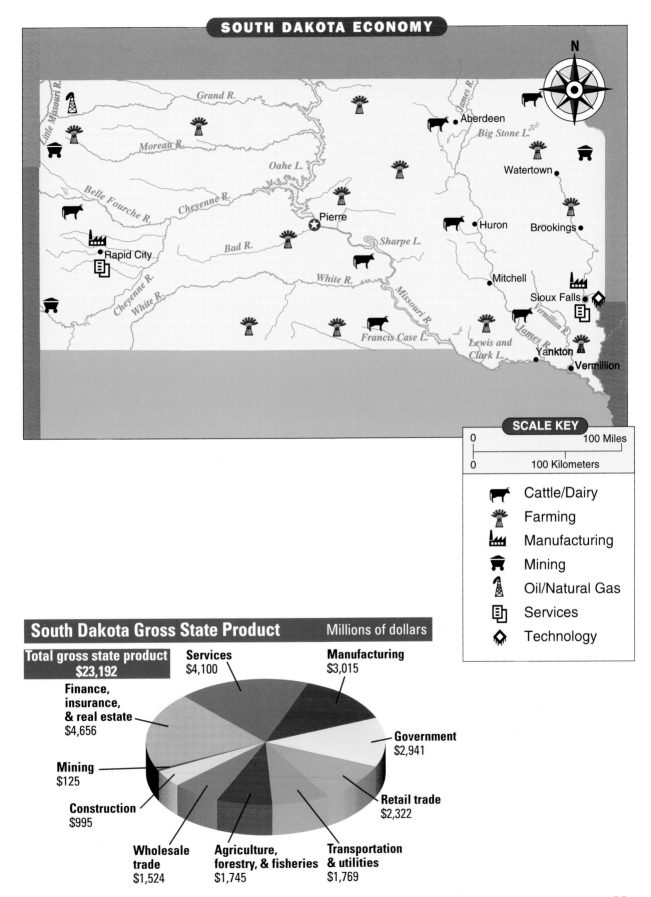

SOUTH DAKOTA ECONOMY

Little Missouri R.

Grand R.

Moreau R.

Oahe L.

Belle Fourche R.

Cheyenne R.

Bad R.

Rapid City

Cheyenne R.

White R.

White R.

Pierre

Sharpe L.

Aberdeen

Big Stone L.

Watertown

Huron

Brookings

Mitchell

Missouri R.

Francis Case L.

Lewis and Clark L.

Vermillion R.

James R.

Sioux Falls

Yankton

Vermillion

SCALE KEY

0   100 Miles

0   100 Kilometers

- Cattle/Dairy
- Farming
- Manufacturing
- Mining
- Oil/Natural Gas
- Services
- Technology

South Dakota Gross State Product

Millions of dollars

Total gross state product $23,192

Services $4,100

Manufacturing $3,015

Finance, insurance, & real estate $4,656

Government $2,941

Mining $125

Retail trade $2,322

Construction $995

Wholesale trade $1,524

Agriculture, forestry, & fisheries $1,745

Transportation & utilities $1,769

government sector, as are the state's public school teachers.

Tourism is another important service industry in South Dakota. More than six million people travel to the state each year, mostly to see Mount Rushmore and the state's national parks. In 2001, tourism generated nearly $1.3 billion in economic activity for South Dakota.

Manufacturing

After services, manufacturing is the most important sector of South Dakota's economy. Manufacturing activities contributed 13 percent of the gross state product in 2000. The state's main durable product (anything meant to last three years or more) is industrial machinery, including farm equipment, aircraft parts, and truck trailers. Electronic equipment and instruments, including computers and scientific supplies, are also important to the state's economy.

South Dakota's most important nondurable product (anything meant to last less than three years) is food products. Meat processing and packing, dairy processing, and poultry processing make major contributions to South Dakota's economy.

Agriculture and Mining

Although agriculture is no longer the mainstay of South Dakota's economy, it is still a vital part of the state's lifestyle. Farms and ranch land cover roughly 90 percent of South Dakota's land area. Together with forests and fisheries, agricultural businesses contributed 7.5 percent of the gross state product in 2000. Just over half of the state's agricultural income today comes from livestock, including cattle and calves, hogs, and sheep. The rest comes from crops, including corn, soybeans, oats, wheat, sunflowers, and sorghum.

Mining is a small part of South Dakota's economy. In 2000, this sector provided just 0.5 percent of the gross state product. Nonmetallic minerals such as clay, limestone, and granite are the state's most important mined products. Gold mines also operate in South Dakota but make a smaller contribution to the state's economy.

Transportation and Communications

South Dakota is off the beaten path for most travelers. Thanks to an efficient transportation network, however, it is easy to travel to and within the state. Interstate 29 in the eastern part of the state is the major north-south route. Interstate 90 in the lower half of the state is South Dakota's major east-west route and is also an important U.S. artery, running from Massachusetts to the state of Washington.

South Dakota is also connected to the rest of the United States and the world by trains and airplanes. A number of railway lines give access to trains that bring freight into and out of South Dakota. Meanwhile, two major airports, Joe Foss Field in Sioux Falls and Rapid City Regional Airport, handle air traffic into and out of the state. Many smaller airstrips handle local flights.

South Dakota is a large state, and in most areas its population is spread thin. Isolated South Dakotans keep in touch with their state and the rest of the world through an extensive radio, TV, and newspaper network. The state has about 130 newspapers, of which 11 are dailies. The largest dailies are the Sioux Falls *Argus Leader*, with a circulation of 55,500, and the *Rapid City Journal*, with a circulation of 36,500. Nearly 120 radio stations broadcast every kind of music, news, and talk imaginable, and 27 television stations bring the world into South Dakotans' homes.

▲ South Dakota is crisscrossed by long, empty stretches of highway. A traveler can go for miles without seeing another vehicle.

Made in South Dakota

Leading farm products and crops
Corn
Soybeans
Oats
Wheat
Sunflowers
Sorghum
Sheep
Cattle and calves
Hogs

Other products
Industrial machinery
Processed foods
Electronic equipment and instruments
Motor vehicles

Major Airports		
Airport	Location	Passengers per year (2000)
Joe Foss Field	Sioux Falls	720,671
Rapid City Regional	Rapid City	392,939

Daily Operations

> All men are born equally free and independent, and have certain inherent rights. . . . To secure these rights governments are instituted among men, deriving their just powers from the consent of the governed.
>
> — *South Dakota State Constitution, 1889*

South Dakota's state constitution was adopted in 1889. The document has been amended many times, however, to address changing conditions of life in the state.

South Dakota's constitution is progressive in that it gives citizens, not just legislators, the right to make laws. To propose a law, at least 5 percent of the state's citizens must sign a petition. All of the state's citizens then vote on the proposed law. If the law passes, it may not be vetoed (rejected) by the governor.

South Dakota's constitution also shows the state's agricultural roots. The document allows the state government to oversee such things as hail insurance and the drainage and irrigation of agricultural lands. It also gives government the power to establish flour mills and packing houses as necessary for the good of the state.

The system of government in South Dakota — just like that of the U.S. federal government — is divided into three branches: executive, legislative, and judicial. The executive branch administers laws, the legislative branch makes laws, and the judicial branch interprets and enforces laws. In addition to the state government, South Dakota has nine Native tribes with their own federally recognized governments.

The Executive Branch

South Dakota's executive branch includes the governor, lieutenant governor, attorney general, secretary of state,

State Constitution

"We, the people of South Dakota, grateful to Almighty God for our civil and religious liberties, in order to form a more perfect and independent government, establish justice, insure tranquility, provide for the common defense, promote the general welfare and preserve to ourselves and to our posterity the blessings of liberty, do ordain and establish this constitution for the state of South Dakota."

— *Preamble to the 1889 South Dakota State Constitution*

Elected Posts in the Executive Branch

Office	Length of Term	Term Limits
Governor	4 years	2 consecutive terms
Lieutenant Governor	4 years	2 consecutive terms
Attorney General	4 years	2 consecutive terms
Secretary of State	4 years	2 consecutive terms
Auditor	4 years	2 consecutive terms
Treasurer	4 years	2 consecutive terms
Commissioner of School and Public Lands	4 years	2 consecutive terms

auditor, treasurer, and commissioner of school and public lands. Each of these officials is appointed by public election and holds office for a term of four years. These elected officials may serve no more than two consecutive terms.

The governor's main duty is reviewing and either approving or vetoing bills that are passed by the state's legislative branch. The governor is also commander in chief of South Dakota's armed forces and is responsible for overseeing the state's sixteen executive departments, including the departments of Agriculture, Corrections, Health, Revenue, and Tourism.

The Legislative Branch

South Dakota's legislative branch is called the South Dakota Legislature. It includes the senate, with thirty-five members, and the house of representatives, with seventy members. State senators and representatives can serve no more than four consecutive two-year terms.

The state legislature meets each year in Pierre, South Dakota's state capital. In even-numbered years the legislature meets for thirty-five working days. In odd-numbered years it meets for forty working days. The governor may call special sessions at other times if necessary.

During a legislative session, senators and representatives create new laws.

▼ The capitol in Pierre houses the South Dakota Legislature.

Laws start out as bills that must be voted on by both the house and the senate. If a bill is passed by both bodies, it is given to the governor for approval or veto.

The Judicial Branch

South Dakota's judicial branch is called the Unified Judicial System, or UJS. The UJS interprets and enforces the laws of the state. It is a three-level system that includes a supreme court, circuit courts, and magistrate courts.

The supreme court is the highest level of South Dakota's judicial branch. Its main job is to review the rulings of the state's lower courts. The supreme court has five members — a chief justice and four associate justices. Supreme court justices are appointed by the governor but are subject to a general election three years after they take office and every eight years thereafter. At these elections, voters decide whether to keep or reject a justice who is up for reelection.

Immediately below the supreme court are the circuit courts. South Dakota has seven judicial circuits with a total of thirty-eight judges, who are elected by voters to eight-year terms. The circuit courts are the general trial courts of the UJS. They try felony cases and civil cases involving more than $10,000 in damages.

The lowest level of the UJS is the magistrate courts. These courts help the circuit courts by processing minor criminal cases and less serious civil actions. They may also perform marriages, issue warrants, and handle other simple legal matters.

Local and Tribal Governments

At the local level, South Dakota is split into sixty-six counties. Each county is responsible for its own elections, collection of taxes, law enforcement, and other local matters. Counties are governed by boards of three to five commissioners, who are elected by voters to four-year terms.

South Dakota also has nine federally recognized Native tribes, all of which are part of the Sioux nation. These

| Legislature | | | |
House	Number of Members	Length of Term	Term Limits
Senate	35 senators	2 years	4 consecutive terms
House of Representatives	70 representatives	2 years	4 consecutive terms

tribes are not bound by state laws. Instead, they are under the direct supervision of the U.S. government. Each tribe has the same power as a state to make its own laws. The tribes communicate with South Dakota's state government through the Office of Tribal Government Relations. This office is run by a Native commissioner who acts as a liaison between the state and tribal government offices.

The National Picture

Like all U.S. states, South Dakota has two members in the U.S. Senate. It has just one member in the U.S. House of Representatives. U.S. senators are elected to six-year terms and representatives are elected to two-year terms. There are no term limits for members of the U.S. Congress.

Historically, South Dakotans have voted in favor of the Republican Party. More than 70 percent of the state's national Congressional representatives have been Republicans. In 2000, Republican presidential candidate George W. Bush earned 60 percent of South Dakota's votes, easily defeating Democratic challenger Al Gore.

HHH

Hubert Horatio Humphrey, Jr., was born in Wallace, South Dakota, in 1911. He spent his childhood in Doland until he moved to Minnesota to attend college. Humphrey began his political career as the mayor of Minneapolis, Minnesota. He was elected to the U.S. Senate from Minnesota in 1948, and served as a Senator until 1964. HHH, as he became known, gave up his Senate seat in 1964 when he was elected vice president of the United States. He served as the second highest elected official in the country until January 1969. Humphrey was the Democratic Party's nominee for president in 1968, but he narrowly lost the election to Richard M. Nixon. He concluded his political career when he returned to the Senate in 1971, where he served until his death in 1978. Humphrey was known as a champion of civil rights, federal medical insurance for seniors, and limits on nuclear weapons.

....

▼ **The South Dakota house of representatives debates legislation in the state capitol in Pierre.**

History, Arts, and Outdoors

> In the vicinity of Harney Peak, in the Black Hills of South Dakota are opportunities for heroic sculpture of unusual character. Would it be possible for you to design and supervise a massive sculpture there? . . . I feel quite sure we could arrange to finance such an enterprise.
>
> — *South Dakota Department of History superintendent Doane Robinson in a letter to sculptor Gutzon Borglum, 1924*

Many residents in certain regions of South Dakota live far from the state's big cities, so urban-style entertainment opportunities are limited for much of South Dakota's population.

Such opportunities do exist, however, in South Dakota's most densely populated areas. Residents who travel to Sioux Falls or other major cities can take advantage of theatrical productions, symphonies, and other cultural events. Meanwhile, those who do not get to the cities much can enjoy outdoor activities, historic attractions, sports, and more. Residents and visitors alike find plenty to do in the Mount Rushmore State.

The Great Outdoors

One of South Dakota's biggest draws is its wide variety of natural treasures. Many of these treasures are on display at the state's national parks and forests. More than a million tourists visit the state's Badlands National Park each year to admire the area's cliffs, spires, canyons, and other rocky formations. The Black Hills National Forest

DID YOU KNOW?

Long before white settlers arrived in the South Dakota region, the area's Sioux residents called the Badlands "mako sica," which means "bad land."

▶ South Dakota residents and visitors enjoy horseback riding in the spectacular Black Hills region.

is another popular destination. Hikers, mountain bikers, and horseback riders can travel through the area on the 111-mile (179-km) Centennial Trail, which runs north to south through the entire forest area.

South Dakota's impressive cave system is the main attraction at Wind Cave National Park and Jewel Cave National Monument in the Black Hills. Wind Cave is the world's seventh-longest cave, and Jewel Cave ranks third. Visitors can take underground tours to see the caves' stalagmites, stalactites, and other wonders.

Wind Cave National Park and adjoining Custer State Park are also famous for their herds of free-roaming bison. People driving through these parks are sometimes forced to stop their cars when they come across bison standing in the road. In South Dakota, this situation is known as a "buffalo jam."

Besides exploring South Dakota's national parks and forests, people can find plenty of other ways to enjoy the outdoors. Many state residents and visitors enjoy boating, hunting, fishing, hiking, horseback riding, and camping around central South Dakota's "Great Lakes" (Oahe, Francis Case, Sharpe, and Lewis and Clark). During the wintertime,

Carving Mount Rushmore

The magnificent Mount Rushmore National Memorial took fourteen years to carve and cost approximately $900,000. Mount Rushmore was chosen as the site of the monument because of its height and the soft consistency of its granite. Sculptor and project manager Gutzon Borglum also liked the rock face's southeastern exposure, which received direct sunlight for most of the day. The monument was originally supposed to show full busts of Presidents Washington, Jefferson, Roosevelt, and Lincoln. However, carving work stopped after Borglum's death in 1941, when only the presidents' faces were complete. No further work is planned.

residents and visitors also enjoy snow skiing at the Terry Peak and Deer Mountain ski areas near the town of Lead.

History on Display

Natural attractions make South Dakota special, but the state's historical attractions have made it famous. The imposing Mount Rushmore National Memorial is a particular favorite among tourists. Carved out of a granite mountain, this monument shows the sixty-foot-high (18.3-meter-high) faces of U.S. presidents George Washington, Thomas Jefferson, Theodore Roosevelt, and Abraham Lincoln.

The success of Mount Rushmore has inspired a second carved stone monument. Sculptors are currently working on the Crazy Horse Memorial near the town of Custer. When complete, the monument will show Sioux warrior Crazy Horse riding a stallion and pointing toward the Black Hills. It will be 563 feet (172 m) high and 641 feet (195 m) long, making it the world's largest statue. Today, visitors can watch the work in progress on this enormous carving, which was started in 1948. Officials will not guess at a finish date for the memorial, but the carving probably will not be completed for many years or even decades to come.

DID YOU KNOW?

The book *Bury My Heart at Wounded Knee* by Dee Brown, first published in 1971, describes U.S. history from the Native point of view. Ending with an account of the Wounded Knee massacre, this groundbreaking book brought attention to the U.S. government's historic mistreatment and exploitation of Native peoples.

A portion of South Dakota's Native heritage is on display at the Prehistoric Indian Village in Mitchell. This attraction preserves a town site where about a thousand Natives lived around one thousand years ago. More recent events are recalled at the Wounded Knee Massacre Memorial, where gravestones and a carved pillar mark the site of the 1890 massacre of nearly three hundred Sioux by U.S. troops.

South Dakota's rugged early days can be relived at historic Fort Sisseton near Lake City and Fort Meade Cavalry Museum in Sturgis. Both sites feature preserved fort buildings and historic artifacts. The town of Deadwood, once one of the West's wildest mining towns, is also a major attraction. Old-time saloons, shops, and casinos capture the town's frontier spirit while well-preserved buildings, streets, and churches give visitors a taste of the Old West.

Fans of writer Laura Ingalls Wilder will not want to miss the Surveyors' Shanty and the Ingalls House in De Smet. The Surveyors' Shanty was the Ingalls family's first house in De Smet; the wood-frame Ingalls House was hand-built by Pa Ingalls himself.

▼ Deadwood's well-preserved historic district gives visitors a taste of the Old West.

Museums and Arts

South Dakota has a number of fine museums, many of which display artifacts from the state's past. The earth-covered South Dakota Cultural Heritage Center in Pierre features exhibits about the state's pioneer and Native history. The Sioux Indian Museum and the Minnelusa Pioneer Museum in Rapid City show traditional and contemporary Native art and historic artifacts. The Old Courthouse Museum in Sioux Falls explores the history of the local area.

▲ The Journey Museum in Rapid City details the life of the Lakota and the pioneers who shared it.

In Vermillion, visitors and residents enjoy the unusual National Music Museum on the campus of the University of South Dakota. Known as one of the world's finest music museums, it houses over ten thousand musical instruments from different cultures and time periods.

Contemporary art is the main feature at the South Dakota Art Museum on the Brookings campus of South Dakota State University. Changing exhibits at this museum show the work of various artists. Contemporary art is also the focus of the Oscar Howe Art Center in Mitchell, where many paintings by Howe, South Dakota's best-known Native artist, are on display.

People who enjoy the performing arts can find much to enjoy at the Washington Pavilion of Arts and Science in Sioux Falls. Completed in 1999, this state-of-the-art facility hosts theatrical productions, symphony orchestras, dance troupes, and other cultural events.

Sports, Zoos, and Oddities

South Dakota has no major league sports teams. The state does, however, have several minor league teams, all based in Sioux Falls. Sports-loving residents enjoy attending Canaries (Northern League) baseball games, Skyforce (Continental Basketball Association) basketball games,

DID YOU KNOW?

The Triple U Buffalo Ranch in central South Dakota was the setting for the Academy Award-winning movie *Dances With Wolves* (1990), starring Kevin Costner.

SpitFire (United Soccer Leagues) soccer games, Stampede (U.S. Hockey League) hockey games, and Storm (National Indoor Football League) football games.

Sioux Falls is also the home of the Great Plains Zoo. In Sherman Park, it houses about four hundred animals, including flamingoes, Asian cats, zebras, and penguins. The zoo is also the home of the Delbridge Museum of Natural History, where more than 150 animal artifacts are on display.

For those seeking quirkier entertainment, the Corn Palace in Mitchell may be just the ticket. The outside of this unusual building is covered with murals made of multicolored corn, oats, barley, and other grains. It takes approximately three thousand bushels of corn to create the murals, which are changed every year.

Wall Drug in the town of Wall is another unique place. Once a tiny drug store, this remote stopping post became popular in the late 1930s by offering free ice water to travelers and advertising all over the world. Today Wall Drug covers an entire city block and employs about one-third of all Wall residents. The store features two animatronic cowboy bands in addition to food, crafts, books, jewelry, and, of course, a pharmacy.

Making the Murals

Creating the multigrain murals that cover the Corn Palace is a painstaking job. First, local artists design the murals in miniature. Then the designs are enlarged and transferred onto giant pieces of paper in outline form. After the huge outlines are tacked to the walls of the Corn Palace, workers fill in the blanks with the appropriate colors of corn and other grains. Before being attached to the wall, each ear of corn is sliced in half with a power saw and hand-trimmed, if necessary, with an axe. It is then nailed in place.

The images "painted in corn" are usually related to life in South Dakota. Wagon trains, farm scenes, and Native activities are typical mural topics.

Left: This image of a man riding a bull is one of the murals on the walls of the Corn Palace.

Faces of the West

> Like the early glaciers that carved out our land, the events and people of South Dakota have shaped what we are today.
> — *U.S. Senator Tom Daschle, 2002*

Following are only a few of the thousands of people who were born, died, or spent much of their lives in South Dakota and made extraordinary contributions to the state and the nation.

SITTING BULL
SIOUX LEADER

BORN: *1831, Grand River*
DIED: *December 15, 1890, Grand River*

As a young man, Sitting Bull showed his bravery in battle. However, he chose to become a medicine man and political leader rather than a war chief. He eventually became so well respected among the Sioux that he was given authority over several subtribes — a highly unusual move for the independent Sioux. Sitting Bull was known for his resistance to U.S. government policies. He is probably best remembered for his participation in the Battle of the Little Bighorn in 1876, at which Lieutenant Colonel George Armstrong Custer and more than two hundred U.S. soldiers lost their lives. In 1890, Sitting Bull was arrested by tribal police who feared that he would lead an uprising. A fight followed during which Sitting Bull was shot and killed.

BLACK ELK
SIOUX MEDICINE MAN

BORN: *December 1863, Little Powder River, WY*
DIED: *August 17, 1950, Pine Ridge Reservation*

Black Elk was a respected Sioux shaman, or medicine man. In 1931, Black Elk was interviewed by poet and writer John Neihardt. The shaman's words were later published in the book *Black Elk Speaks: The Life Story of a Holy Man of the Oglala Sioux*. Other interviews in the late 1940s resulted in a book called *The Sacred Pipe,* which revealed details of many traditional Sioux religious rituals. These two books are among the world's most important chronicles of Native American life.

LAURA INGALLS WILDER

WRITER

BORN: *February 7, 1867, Pepin, WI*
DIED: *February 10, 1957, Mansfield, MO*

Born in Wisconsin, Laura Ingalls moved with her family to Dakota Territory in 1879. The Ingalls family spent many years living near the town of De Smet. Later in life, Wilder decided to write about her childhood on the American frontier. Her first children's book, *Little House in the Big Woods*, was such a huge success that Wilder was encouraged to write others. Many titles, including *Little House on the Prairie*, *On the Banks of Plum Creek*, and *By the Shores of Silver Lake*, followed. Wilder's books today are considered classics and are loved by children and adults around the world.

HARVEY DUNN

ILLUSTRATOR

BORN: *March 8, 1884, Manchester*
DIED: *October 29, 1952, Tenafly, NJ*

Harvey Dunn is considered one of the most important American illustrators of the early twentieth century. He was especially well known for his pictures in *The Saturday Evening Post* over a thirty-five-year period. Dunn also produced illustrations for book publishers; other magazines such as

Cosmopolitan, *Harper's Weekly*, and *Scribner's Monthly*; and corporations such as Coca-Cola, Maxwell House Coffee, and Texaco. In addition to his huge body of work, Dunn is also remembered as a great teacher of illustration.

EARL SANDE

JOCKEY

BORN: *November 13, 1898, Groton*
DIED: *August 20, 1968, Jacksonville, OR*

South Dakota native Earl Sande began his career as a professional jockey in 1918. He immediately established a reputation as one of horse racing's top riders. He was the sport's leading money winner in 1921, 1923, and 1927. He is

also one of only ten jockeys to have won the Triple Crown (a three-race series consisting of the Kentucky Derby, the Preakness Stakes, and the Belmont Stakes). In honor of his contributions to the sport of horse racing, Sande was inducted into the National Museum of Racing's Hall of Fame in 1955.

ERNEST O. LAWRENCE

PHYSICIST

BORN: *August 8, 1901, Canton*
DIED: *August 27, 1958, Palo Alto, CA*

Physicist Ernest O. Lawrence is best known for his invention of the cyclotron, a device that accelerates atomic particles. During World War II, the cyclotron was essential to the development of the nuclear bomb. Lawrence was awarded the Nobel Prize in Physics in 1939 for his work.

Ben Reifel

BORN: *September 19, 1906, Parmelee*
DIED: *January 2, 1990, Sioux Falls*

As the son of a white father and a Sioux mother, Ben Reifel grew up understanding both cultures. In 1946, he put this knowledge to work by becoming the first District Tribal Relations Officer for the northern Great Plains states. In this position, Reifel gained valuable experience as a mediator between U.S. government bodies and Native tribes. In 1961, Reifel became the first member of the Sioux Nation to be elected to the U.S. House of Representatives. He served in Congress until his retirement in 1971.

Oscar Howe

BORN: *May 13, 1915, Joe Creek*
DIED: *October 7, 1983, Vermillion*

Sioux painter Oscar Howe was among the first Native Americans to use modern techniques in his work. His use of cubism and other abstract methods to show traditional Native activities brought new excitement to old subjects. Howe's fight to earn acceptance for his work also changed the way people thought about Native American art. Today, much of Howe's work is on display at the Oscar Howe Art Center in Mitchell.

Bob Barker

BORN: *December 12, 1923, Darrington, WA*

Born in Washington, Bob Barker spent most of his youth on South Dakota's Rosebud Indian Reservation, where his

mother was a schoolteacher. After attending college in Missouri, Barker got a job at a radio station and soon had his own program, *The Bob Barker Show*. Later he was hired as the host of the popular game show *Truth or Consequences*. He held this job for eighteen years before moving on to host *The Price Is Right*, which was to become one of the best-loved game shows of all time. Barker has won eleven Emmy awards as a TV host, more than any other performer. He has also earned two Emmys as executive producer of *The Price Is Right* plus an Emmy for lifetime achievement, for a total of fourteen career Emmys.

Allen Neuharth

BORN: *March 22, 1924, Eureka*

As a young man, Allen Neuharth began his career in journalism by working for the Associated Press in South Dakota. Over the years, he held a series of increasingly important positions at different news organizations. In 1963, Neuharth joined the Gannett Company, which owned many newspapers across the nation. By 1973, Neuharth had become Gannett's president and chief executive officer. Under Neuharth's leadership, Gannett was transformed into the largest newspaper publisher in the United States, with annual revenues of more than $3 billion. Neuharth's greatest success at Gannett was the launch of *USA Today*, which today is the nation's best-selling newspaper.

SPARKY ANDERSON
ATHLETE

BORN: *February 22, 1934, Bridgewater*

Athlete George "Sparky" Anderson began his professional baseball career in 1953 as an infielder in the Brooklyn Dodgers farm system. He later played in the major league for just one year (1959) with the Philadelphia Phillies before moving to the international league in Toronto. Anderson found his real calling when he became a team manager in 1964. During his career, Anderson managed the Cincinnati Reds and the Detroit Tigers. He was chosen to manage National League All-Star teams four times between 1971 and 1977 and was twice named Manager of the Year. He was inducted into the Baseball Hall of Fame in 2000.

BILLY MILLS
ATHLETE

BORN: *June 30, 1938, Pine Ridge Reservation*

Sioux track and field star Billy Mills is best known for earning a gold medal in the ten-thousand-meter race in the 1964 Olympics. Two other runners were favored to take first and second place in the event, but Mills came from behind to win, and set an Olympic speed record in the process. Mills later worked to reestablish the American Indian Athletic Hall of Fame. His story was memorialized in the 1983 film *Running Brave*.

TOM BROKAW
BROADCAST JOURNALIST

BORN: *February 6, 1940, Webster*

After graduating from the University of South Dakota in 1962, Tom Brokaw landed a job as a morning news editor and newscaster with a TV station in Omaha, Nebraska. A variety of increasingly important TV jobs followed. In 1976, Brokaw was offered a cohost position on NBC's *Today* show. He held that job until 1982, when he returned to serious journalism as coanchor of the *NBC Nightly News*. The show's cohost Roger Mudd soon stepped down, leaving Brokaw as the solo newsman. Brokaw still hosts the *NBC Nightly News* and has earned a reputation for down-home charm and an ability to ad-lib during interviews.

CHERYL LADD
ACTRESS

BORN: *July 12, 1951, Huron*

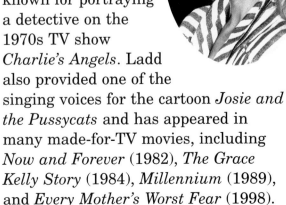

Born Cheryl Jean Stoppelmoor, actress Cheryl Ladd is best known for portraying a detective on the 1970s TV show *Charlie's Angels*. Ladd also provided one of the singing voices for the cartoon *Josie and the Pussycats* and has appeared in many made-for-TV movies, including *Now and Forever* (1982), *The Grace Kelly Story* (1984), *Millennium* (1989), and *Every Mother's Worst Fear* (1998).

South Dakota

History At-A-Glance

1500–1700s
Ancestors of present-day Native peoples arrive in the South Dakota area.

1803
Napoleon Bonaparte sells the Louisiana Territory to the United States.

1817
French trader Joseph La Framboise opens Fort Tecumseh (later called Fort Pierre), the South Dakota region's first permanent trading post.

1851
The Laramie Treaty assigns 60 million acres (24,282,000 ha) of land to the Sioux and establishes tribal borders.

1862
The Homestead Act encourages the settlement of Dakota Territory by promising settlers 160 acres (65 ha) of free land.

1868
The Fort Laramie Treaty establishes the Great Sioux Reservation and gives the Sioux some Dakota Territory land.

1743
Brothers François and Louis Joseph de La Vérendrye are probably the first Europeans to explore the South Dakota area.

1804–06
Lewis and Clark's Expedition travels from Missouri to the Pacific Ocean and back, crossing the South Dakota region twice.

1831
The steamboat *Yellowstone* begins making regular trips to Fort Tecumseh.

1861
The U.S. Congress establishes Dakota Territory.

1862
Dakota Territory establishes a public school system.

1873
A proposed Northern Pacific Railway route through the Black Hills sparks conflict between the Sioux and settlers.

1600   **1700**   **1800**

1492
Christopher Columbus comes to New World.

1607
Capt. John Smith and three ships land on Virginia coast and start first English settlement in New World — Jamestown.

1754–63
French and Indian War.

1773
Boston Tea Party.

1776
Declaration of Independence adopted July 4.

1777
Articles of Confederation adopted by Continental Congress.

1787
U.S. Constitution written.

1812–14
War of 1812.

United States
History At-A-Glance

1874
The Great Dakota Boom begins when prospectors flock to South Dakota after reports of gold appear in a Chicago newspaper.

1889
The Great Sioux Agreement establishes six reservation areas within South Dakota and opens up new land to non-Native settlement.

1889
South Dakota becomes the fortieth U.S. state.

1917–18
American participation in World War I boosts South Dakota's economy.

1930s
The Great Depression has a severe effect on the South Dakota economy.

1973
The American Indian Movement holds a rally on South Dakota's Pine Ridge Reservation to protest the poor living conditions of Native Americans.

1879–90
Laura Ingalls Wilder lives in the town of De Smet, which she later features in four of her books.

1889
South Dakota adopts its first state constitution.

1890
U.S. troops kill nearly three hundred Natives at Wounded Knee.

1927
Sculptor Gutzon Borglum begins work on the Mount Rushmore National Memorial.

1941–45
Demand for agricultural goods increases when America enters World War II, making South Dakota's economy rebound.

1980
The U.S. Supreme Court rules that land was illegally seized from the Sioux in 1876 and orders repayment.

1800　　　　　　　　　**1900**　　　　　　　　　**2000**

1848
Gold discovered in California draws eighty thousand prospectors in the 1849 Gold Rush.

1869
Transcontinental railroad completed.

1929
Stock market crash ushers in Great Depression.

1950–53
U.S. fights in the Korean War.

2000
George W. Bush wins the closest presidential election in history.

1861–65
Civil War.

1917–18
U.S. involvement in World War I.

1941–45
U.S. involvement in World War II.

1964–73
U.S. involvement in Vietnam War.

2001
A terrorist attack in which four hijacked airliners crash into New York City's World Trade Center, the Pentagon, and farmland in western Pennsylvania leaves thousands dead or injured.

▼ Government agents distribute the annual supply of goods to the Assiniboines in return for their withdrawal to a reservation between the Missouri and Yellowstone Rivers. This agreement was drawn up in the Fort Laramie Treaty of 1851.

Something for Everyone

Check web site for exact date and directions.

Black Hills Pow Wow,
Rapid City

The main attractions of this traditional pow wow are the dance competitions. Accompanied by drums, Native dancers of all ages perform in categories including Jingle Dress, Fancy Shawl, Grass, and Fancy Bustle. The event also includes a Native art expo.
www.blackhillspowwow.com

Black Hills Roundup,
Belle Fourche

More than eighty years old, this event features area cowboys and cowgirls competing in bull riding, bronc busting, and other traditional rodeo favorites. Musical entertainment and a carnivalare also part of this five-day Western blowout.
www.bellefourche.org/roundup.htm

Buffalo Roundup,
Custer State Park

Watch the action as park staff, cowboys, and cowgirls saddle up to move the park's fifteen hundred bison into corrals. Once captured, some of the bison are freed; others are sold at auction.
www.custerstatepark.info/round.htm

Corn Palace Festival,
Mitchell

This annual event celebrates all things related to corn. Visitors can admire the finished murals decorating the Corn Palace's walls. Event features a carnival, musical concerts, and, of course, plenty of fresh corn to eat.
www.cornpalacefestival.com

Czech Days, Tabor

This annual festival celebrates Tabor's Czech roots with traditional food, polka music, dancing, and more. Take home some traditional Czech dolls or tasty kolaches (pastries) handmade by one of Tabor's Czech descendants.
www.byelectric.com/~tabor

Days of '76, Deadwood

A carnival, street dances, free concerts, and parades are all part of this celebration, which commemorates Deadwood's gold rush days. The event also includes a rodeo that won the Professional Rodeo Cowboys Association's Small Outdoor Rodeo of the Year award four years running.
www.deadwood.org/events.htm

Gold Discovery Days, Custer

This long-running event celebrates the discovery of gold in the Black Hills with a parade, a carnival, an art fair, and more.
www.custersd.com/events.asp?EV_TYPE=1

Laura Ingalls Wilder Pageant, De Smet

Actors re-create events in the life of famed author Laura Ingalls Wilder. Ma and Pa Ingalls, sisters Mary, Carrie, and Grace, and young Laura come alive in faithfully executed scenes from Wilder's beloved books. www.ingallshomestead.com/links/desmet/pageant.html

Lewis and Clark Spirit Mound Festival, Vermillion

On August 25, 1804, Lewis and Clark climbed Spirit Mound, an isolated hill near present-day Vermillion. The popular Spirit Mound Festival celebrates this climb through historic reenactments, keelboat races, Native art exhibitions, and a pow wow. www.travelsd.com/events/GE/lc_smound.htm

Motorcycle Rally and Races, Sturgis

About 300,000 motorcycle enthusiasts take over the town of Sturgis each year during this rally, which is one of the world's largest. The event includes races, concerts, and more. www.rally.sturgis.sd.us

Northern Plains Tribal Arts Festival, Sioux Falls

Each year this juried art show features the work of some of the nation's best Native American artists. www.aistribalarts.com

▶ Bikers from all over the United States attend the Sturgis Motorcycle Rally and Races each summer.

Rosebud Fair, Rosebud

Held on the Rosebud Indian Reservation, this event includes a traditional pow wow plus an all-Native rodeo, a carnival, and more. www.sdpb.org/DakotaLife/prairiedays/rose.htm

South Dakota Highland Festival, Scotland

Traditional Scottish athletic events, sheepdog exhibitions, bagpipes, and tartan displays are featured at this celebration of Scottish heritage. www.scotlandsd.org/HighlandFest.htm

South Dakota State Fair, Huron

This weeklong event includes a carnival, food, concerts, livestock judging, and other traditional state fair attractions. www.sdstatefair.com/index.asp

Summer Art Festival, Brookings

South Dakota's largest summer arts show features more than two hundred artisans and craftspeople from all over the United States. www.bsaf.com

Books

Bull, Jacqueline Left Hand. *Lakota Hoop Dancer*. New York: Dutton Children's Books, 1999. Learn about Kevin Locke, a Lakota Sioux dancer who performs the traditional hoop dance all over the world.

Freedman, Russell. *Buffalo Hunt*. New York: Holiday House, 1988. Contains vivid accounts of the Great Plains Natives' bison hunts.

Presnall, Judith Janda. *Mount Rushmore*. San Diego: Lucent Books, 2000. Describes the conception, planning, and carving of Mount Rushmore National Memorial.

Schanzer, Rosalyn. *How We Crossed the West: The Adventures of Lewis and Clark*. Washington, D.C.: National Geographic Society, 1997. This simplified version of Lewis and Clark's diaries follows the Expedition throughout its three-year exploration of the West.

Toht, David W. *Sodbuster*. Minneapolis: Lerner Publications, 1995. Excerpts from personal letters and newspapers of the nineteenth century, plus color illustrations, show how the pioneers of South Dakota lived.

Wilder, Laura Ingalls. Edited by Rose Wilder Lane. *On the Way Home: The Diary of a Trip from South Dakota to Mansfield, Missouri, in 1894*. New York: HarperCollins, 1994. This book is a personal diary kept by the author as she and her family traveled from De Smet, South Dakota, to Missouri.

Web Sites

▶ Official state web site
www.state.sd.us

▶ South Dakota travel information
www.travelsd.com

▶ South Dakota State Historical Society
www.sdhistory.org

Films and Documentaries

Costner, Kevin. *Dances With Wolves*. MGM/UA Studios, 1990. This Academy Award-winning movie tells the story of Lieutenant John Dunbar, who travels to Dakota Territory and befriends a Lakota Sioux tribe.

Note: Page numbers in *italics* refer to maps, illustrations, or photographs.

A

Aberdeen, SD, 6
Abourezk, James, 7
age distribution, 16
agriculture, 4, 11–12, 14, 15, 24, *25*, 26, 28
airports, 27
American Indian Athletic Hall of Fame, 41
American Indian Movement (AIM), 15, 43
Anderson, Sparky, 41
animal (state), 6, *6*
antelope, 23, *23*
Argus Leader (newspaper), 27
Arikara Indians, 8
art, 36, 37, *37*, 40, 45
attractions, 7, *44*, 44–45, *45*. *See also* culture; parks

B

Back on the Farm (Latza), 24
Badlands, *20*, 21
Badlands National Park, 7, 32
Barker, Bob, 40, *40*
Battle of the Little Bighorn, 38
Belle Fourche, SD, 44
Big Stone Lake, 20
bird (state), 6, *6*
bison, 4, 7, 10, *15*, 23, 33, 44
Black Elk, 38–39
Black Elk Speaks: The Life Story of a Holy Man of the Oglala Sioux (Neihardt), 38
Black Hills
  chinooks of, 22–23
  conflict over, 12, 15, 42
  Crazy Horse Memorial and, 34
  description of, 21
  gold rush in, 9, 13
Black Hills National Forest, 23, *32*, 32–33
Black Hills Pow Wow, 44, *44*
Black Hills Roundup, 44
Black Hills spruce, 6
The Bob Barker Show, 40
Bonaparte, Napoleon, 8–9, 42
Borglum, Gutzon, 32, 33, 43
Brokaw, Tom, 41, *41*
Brookings, SD, 6, 45
Brown, Dee, 34
buffalo. *See* bison
Buffalo Roundup, 44
Burke, Martha "Calamity Jane", 13
Bury My Heart at Wounded Knee (Brown), 34

Bush, George W., 31
By the Shores of Silver Lake (Wilder), 20, 39

C

capital. *See* Pierre, SD
capitol, *29*, *31*
casinos, 18
cattle ranchers, *26*
Centennial Trail, 33
Charlie's Angels (movie), 41
Cheyenne Indians, 8
Chinese ring-necked pheasant, 6, *6*
Christianity, 19
circuit courts, 30
Citicorp, 24
Clark, William, 9, 42
Cleveland, Grover, 14
climate, 21, 22–23
communications, 27
constitution, state, 13, *13*, 28
Corn Palace, 7, 37, *37*
Corn Palace Festival, 44
Corps of Discovery, 9
Costner, Kevin, 36
counties, 30
Crazy Horse Memorial, 34
culture, *32*, 32–37, *33*, *34*, *35*, *36*, *37*
Custer, George Armstrong, 38
Custer National Forest, 23, 33
Custer, SD, 44
Custer State Park, 15, 44
cyclotron, 39
Czech Days, 44

D

Dakota, 8
Dakota Territory, 11–12, 13, 42
dams, 14
Dances With Wolves (movie), 36
Daschle, Tom, 38
Days of '76, 44
Deadwood, SD, 13, *34*, 35, 44
Deer Mountain ski area, 33
Delbridge Museum of Natural History, 37
De Smet, SD, 35, 39, 43, 45
Dunn, Harvey, 39

E

East River region, 21
economy, 4, 14, 24–27, *25*, *26*, 43
education, 18, 19, 42
elevation, 20
events, *44*, 44–45, *45*
executive branch, 28–29

F

Fairburn agate, 6

farms, 26
films, 46
financial services, 24, *25*
fish (state), 6
flag (state), *6*
Flaming Fountain Memorial, 7
flower (state), 6
food products, 26
foreign-born groups, *16*
forests, 23
Fort Laramie Treaty, 12, 42
Fort Meade Cavalry Museum, 35
Fort Sisseton, 35
Fort Tecumseh, 10, 42
fossils, 6, 7, *7*
France, 8

G

Gannett Company, 40
gemstone (state), 6
German heritage, 17
Ghost Dance, 11, 12–13
Gold Discovery Days, 44
gold rush, 13, 27, 43
Gore, Al, 31
government, 24, *25*, 26, 28–31, *29*, *31*. *See also* U.S. government
governor, 28–29
Great Depression, 14, 43
Great Plains Zoo, 37
Great Sioux Agreement, 12, 43
Great Sioux Reservation, 12, 42
gross state product, *25*

H

"Hail! South Dakota" (state song), 6
Hammitt, Deecort, 6
Harney, Hank, 9
Harney Peak, 20, 32
heritage, *16*, 17, *17*
Hickok, Wild Bill, 13
historical attractions, *34*, 34–35
history, 8–15, *9*, *10*, *11*, *12*, *14*, 42–43
Homestake Mining Company, 7
Homestead Act, 11, 42
honeybee, 6, *6*
Houck Ranch, 36
house of representatives, 29–30, *31*
Howe, Oscar, 40
Humphrey, Hubert Horatio, Jr., 31, *31*
Huron, SD, 45
Hutterites, 19

I

immigration, 16

industrial machinery, 26
Ingalls House, 35
insect (state), 6, *6*
interstate highways, *5*, 27, 40

J

Jefferson, Thomas, 7, 9, 17, 34
Jewel Cave National Monument, 33
Joe Foss Field, 27
judicial branch, 30

L

Ladd, Cheryl, 41, *41*
La Framboise, Joseph, 10, 42
Lake Francis Case, 21
Lake Oahe, 21
lakes, 20–21, 33
Lake Sharpe, 21
Lakota, 8
land, *4*, *20–21*, 20–23, *22*, *23*
land area, 6
Laramie Treaty, 11, 42
Latza, Greg, 24
Laura Ingalls Wilder Pageant, 35, *35*, 45
La Vérendrye, François de, 8, 42
La Vérendrye, Louis Joseph de, 8, 42
Lawrence, Ernest O., 39
legislative branch, 29–30
Lewis and Clark Expedition, 9, *9*, 42
Lewis and Clark Lake, 20–21
Lewis and Clark Spirit Mound Festival, 45
Lewis, Meriwether, 9, 42
Lincoln, Abraham, 7, 34
Little House in the Big Woods (Wilder), 39
Little House on the Prairie (Wilder), 35, 39
livestock, 26
locusts, 10
Louisiana Purchase, 8–9
Lutheran church, 19

M

magistrate courts, 30
mammals, 23
Mammoth Site, 7, *7*
Manuel, Moses and Fred, 9
manufacturing, 4, 24, *25*, 26
maps, *5*, *22*, *25*
Mills, Billy, 41, *41*
minerals, 6, 27
mining, 9, 13, *25*, 26–27, 43
Minnelusa Pioneer Museum, 36
Missouri River, 17, 20–21
Mitchell, SD, 36, 37, *37*, 44
Montana, 11

Motorcycle Rally and
    Races, 45, *45*
motto (state), 6
Mount Rushmore National
    Memorial, 6, 7, 33,
    33, 34, 43
Mudd, Roger, 41
museums, 35–36, *36*, 37

N
national representation, 31
Native Americans
    conflict, 4, 10–11, 12
    events, 44, *44*, 45
    government of, 31
    historical attractions,
        34–35
    modern issues of, 15
    museums, 36
    people, 38, *38*, 40, 41, *41*
    population of, *17*, 17–18
    settlement in South
        Dakota, 8
    in time line, 42–43
NBC Nightly News, 41
Neihardt, John, 38
Neuharth, Allen, 40
newspapers, 27, 40
Nixon, Richard M., 31
Norris, Kathleen, 16
Northern Pacific
    Railroad, 12, 42
Northern Plains
    Tribal Arts, 45

O
Office of Tribal Government
    Relations, 31
Old Courthouse Museum, 36
On the Banks of Plum Creek
    (Wilder), 39
Oscar Howe Art Center, 36, 40
outdoors, *32*, 32–33

P
Paha Ska, 17, *17*
Paleo-Indians, 8
parks, 7, 15, *32*, 32–33.
    See also Mount
        Rushmore National
        Memorial
pasqueflower, 6, 23
Peder Victorius (Rölvaag), 8
people, *38*, 38–41, *39*, *40*, *41*
performing arts, 36
Pierre, SD, 6, 7, 29, *29*, 36
Pine Ridge Reservation, 15,
    17, 43
plants, 23
population, 6, 13, *16*,
    16–17, *17*

pow wow, 44, *44*, 45
prairies, 21
Prehistoric Indian Village, 34
Presidential Peace
    Medallion, 17

R
radio stations, 27
railway, 27
rainfall, 21
Rapid City Journal, 27
Rapid City Regional, 27
Rapid City, SD, 6, 16, 21, 36, 44
Reifel, Ben, 40
religion, 19
Remington, Frederic, *9*
Republican party, 31
reservations, 12, 13, 15,
    17–18, 40, 42, 43
rivers, 20, 21
roads, 5, 27, *27*, 40
Robinson, Doane, 32
rodeo, 44, 45
Rölvaag, O.E., 8
Roman Catholic church, 19
Roosevelt, Theodore, 7, 34
Rosebud Fair and Rodeo, 45
Rosebud Indian Reservation,
    40, 45
Running Brave (movie), 41
Russell, Charles Marion, *10*

S
The Sacred Pipe (Brown),
    38–39
Sande, Earl, 39, *39*
*The Saturday Evening
    Post*, 39
Scotland, SD, 45
senate, 29–30
services, 4, 24, *25*, 26
Shrine to Music Museum, 36
Sioux
    conflict, 10–11, 15
    government of, 31
    hunting, *10*
    people, 38, *38*, 40, 41, *41*
    population of, 17–18
    settlement in South
        Dakota, 8
    in time line, 42–43
    Wounded Knee and,
        12–13
    Wovoka and, 11
Sioux Falls, SD, 6, 7, *18*, 21,
    36, 37, 45
Sioux Indian Museum, 36
Sitting Bull, 38, *38*
skiing, 33
slogan (state), 6
small business, 26

snowfall, 21
sodbusters, 11–12, *14*
song (state), 6
South Dakota
    Art Museum, 36
South Dakota Cultural
    Heritage Center, 36
South Dakota Highland
    Festival, 45, *45*
South Dakota Korean and
    Vietnam War
    Memorial, 7
South Dakota Legislature,
    29–30
South Dakota state
    constitution, 28
South Dakota State Fair, 45
South Dakota State
    University, 19, 36
Spirit Mound, 45
A Spiritual Geography
    (Norris), 16
sports, 36–37, 41
statehood, 6, 13–14, 43
Sturgis, SD, 45
Summer Art Festival, 45
supreme court, 30
Surveyors' Shanty, 35

T
Tabor, SD, 44
taxes, 26
television stations, 27
temperature, 21, 23
Terry Peak ski area, 33
The Price Is Right, 40
time line, 42–43
tourism, 4, 26, *32*, 32–33
trade, *25*
traders, 9–10, 42
transportation, *25*, 27
tree (state), 6
triceratops (state fossil), 6
Triple Crown, 39

U
unemployment, 18
Unified Judicial System
    (UJS), 30
Union, 6, 13–14, 43
University of South Dakota,
    19, 41
USA Today, 40
U.S. Congress, 11, 13–14
U.S. government, 8–9, 38
U.S. House of
    Representatives,
    31, 40
U.S. Senate, 7, 31
U.S. Supreme Court, 15, 43

V
Vermillion, SD, 36, 45
voters, 7, 30

W
Wall, SD, 37
Wall Drug Store, *21*, 37
walleye, 6
Washington, George, 7, 34
Washington Pavilion of Arts
    and Science, 36, *36*
Watertown, SD, 6
West River region, 21
Wilder, Laura Ingalls, 20, 35,
    35, 39, *39*, 43, 45
Wind Cave National Park,
    15, 33
winds, 22–23
World War I, 14, 43
World War II, 14, 39, 43
Wounded Knee, 12–13,
    34, 43
Wounded Knee Memorial,
    12, 35
Wovoka (Paiute holy man),
    11, 11
Wyoming, 11

Y
Yankton Treaty, 11
Yellowstone (steamboat),
    10, 42